ECHOES OF THE SKY

AMARJIT KAUR WALIA

notionpress.com

INDIA · SINGAPORE · MALAYSIA

Dedicated to My Parents

My Inspiration

Acknowledgements

I would like to thank everyone at Notionpress who worked tirelessly to publish this book.

I would also like to thank my son, Manu, without whose computer skills I would not have been able to shape this book.

Contents

Contents

Galvanic Dance

A galvanic dance on the stage of sky

Lightning streaks, a fiery display for every eye

In a sudden burst, all is filled with fright

Quick white flash splits the moonless night.

A cosmic ballet, terrific, across the clouds

With thunderous applause that echoes loud

In dark, wild performance by light and sound

With every flash and thunder, their energy doth astound.

Radiant, a streak of fire in the sky

Boom, a rumble of thunder high and nigh

Nature's forces wild, in the sky they race

Through stormy clouds, they find their space.

Hasty fire bolts shining, a mesmerising sight
Illuminating darkness with their refulgent light
Missiles of brilliance, they fiercely dart
Igniting the sky with their sudden spark.

I'm filled with awe at this sight
Zigzag flash, a thrilling invite
Night's sky light, storm's dark core
A magnificent show, a sight to adore.

Each electric bolt kindles the heart
Nature's brushstrokes, a masterpiece of electric art
Though brief in presence, it leaves a trace
A memory etched in time and space.

Nature's Orchestra

Dark clouds gather heavy, lightning splits the sky
Sky screams a thunderclap loud, the storm draws nigh
Nature's grand orchestra, a primal song
Wild and free, a timeless tune echoes deep and long.

Lightning flashes, fierce, bright, and bold
The sky's theatre, a thunderous spectacle unfolds
Rain comes down, the earth's thirst is bound
In this downpour's embrace, drums of nature resound.

Wind is brutally strong and cold, chilling to the bone
It swooshes through the trees, its power unknown
Leaves fall and scatter, branches sway and creak
Announces its arrival, the tempest's shriek.

Glinting flashes illuminate the night

Terrifying thunder-booms blast with bright delight

In the heart of the wild storm where wild forces sway

The beauty of the storm in all its fury, on grand display.

In that moment, in that sound, as lightning strikes the ground

All is in awe, the earth is bound

To powers greater than we know

Dynamic force of nature that loves to show.

Volatile storm lashes everything on its way

Rain, thunder, lightning have their own say

In the realms of nature's great unknown

There's beauty waiting to be known.

An Elemental Song

Blares the sky with a primal delight
Thunder trumpets through the night
The storm's crescendo, an elemental song
Nature's orchestra booms so long.

Fire bolts dance across the sky
Brilliant, dazzling display up high
My voice echoes with pure jubilation
Filling the air with elation's vibration.

In the midst of booming roar
I find the joy not known before
I let it out, an ecstatic release
A feeling of pure bliss, a feeling of peace.

Stormy clouds so dark and deep

Wind yells and the rain beats

Nature's rhythm I do adore

Reveling in the beauty, I explore.

In harmony with nature, I sing

Screaming in joy, my heart takes wing

I sing of the wonder of all that is

Mystery of life and the magic of this.

Breakers of Silence

Summer afternoon slowly gets masked by cloud cover
Cool breeze pushes the dry air
Wind is rising fast, a warning cry
Storm is coming, there's no denying.

Wind picks up, trees submit and bend
Fire bolt and crackly thunder unleash a powerful blend
It shakes the earth with a deafening sound
That fills them all with a fearsome surround.

A storm is about to break, a warning in the air
Thunder rumbles in the distance, sparking awe and fear
Glaring flashes of lightning burst through the inky sky
In this electric dance nature's sound seems to amplify.

Storm approaches swiftly, blocking out the light

A thick veil of darkness falls, the day turns into night

There's a beauty in the storm we can't ignore

The mesmerising moments, we can't abhor.

The storm's intensity reaches its peak, unyielding and unique

A clash of elements, moments truly mystique

This frenzy seems like it'll never end

But remember dear, storms always suspend.

Darkness

Dark clouds gather ominous and still
Air grows heavy, a feeling of chill
A storm is brewing, the tension mounts
As lightning strikes, the earth it counts.

Rain comes down in sheets of grey
The world is filled with chaos and dismay
Lightning crackles, a violent power of nature
The world aglow with its electric signature.

Wind whips, trees shake and sway
Birds fly away to find a safer place to stay
Leaves, they swirl and twirl and spin
As if possessed by a demon.

In flashes of light, the world is revealed

All shadows flee, all secrets unsealed

The beauty and the pain, the joy and the fear

All laid down bare before us, for us to hold dear.

But then the light fades

We are left in dark once again

We know that the light is still there

Waiting to be revealed over again.

Harsh Nor'wester

A sound echoes and beams a sparkling light
In the total black of gloomy night
A clap of thunder shakes the ground
Fiery lightning bolts dance all around.

Beauty of thunder is a sight to behold
Nature's wild euphony, booming and bold
Ominous crash that fills the air
Reminds that nature's power is indeed quite rare.

Thunder rumbles, lightning flashes
Creating a storm that fiercely thrashes
Sky cracks whilst ground shakes
A harsh nor'wester awakes.

Flashes of light that streak the sky

Across the dark expanse, they fly

Storm that's wild, fierce, too free

Is a spectacle that's a wonder to see.

With crackling lightning, thundering cries, nature's fury accrues

It paints the sky with dark, ominous hues

Flashes of lightning illuminate the sky

Revealing nature's wrath, fierce and spry.

A thunderstorm moving fast and wrathful

Unbridled energy, ballistic and ireful

Through rayless clouds, its frenzy displayed

With incessant rain, its strength conveyed.

Rain in Kolkata's Streets

In Kolkata's bustling streets, falls gentle rain so cool
Colourful umbrellas pop up like flowers in bloom
Pitter-patter of raindrops, a melodic serenade
Each note resounding a tune that never wanes.

It washes away the heat of the day
People move quickly on their way
Sound of rain is soothing to the soul
Offering solace and joy, it takes away troubles and woes.

Air is fresher, colours are brighter
A feeling of happiness, life seems sweeter
Scent of wet earth, a soothing embrace
Everything is alive with rain's touch of caress.

Children play and dance in puddles

Soaked to the skin, they enjoy the muddle

They scream in joy as they splash

In children's world, it's a magical flash.

Washed in rain, the city is reborn

Soaked in joy, a world to adorn

Renews the spirit with each drop's dance

Takes the heart on a journey of romance.

Rhapsody in Rain

With rain comes down a gentle mist

The sound it makes, a subtle twist

Each droplet of rain on grass blades so green

Reflects the light with a sparkling sheen.

Pitter-patter of the rain's soft song

Dances on the streets all along

Fills the breeze with earthly perfume

Leaves the world refreshed and renewed.

Streets are alive with joyous sound

It is both soft and loud

It sings of life, of growth, of change

Of seasons passing, of love that wanes.

Rain brings peace to the weary soul

Nourishes the earth to make it whole

Feeds the roots of all small, big trees

Whispers of hope on a gentle breeze.

Rejoice and embrace the rain's cool gift

Revel in the joy that it can lift

It may seem like a simple thing

It has the power to make our hearts sing.

Rain on a Sunny Day

Rain on a sunny day, a wonderful sight to see

A gift from the sky that brings joy to me

A day to enjoy fresh air and sunshine

To go out and make memories that'll last a lifetime.

Sun's warmth is still lingering as drops of rain come down

Birds are singing, leaves are rustling, air is bathed in sound

The union of light and rain creates colours so profound

Sunbeams dance on the droplets, nature's artistry does abound.

Raindrops dance and gleam on leaves and petals fair

Nature's rhythm starts to teem, a sight beyond compare

A welcome sight, time to enjoy peace and tranquillity

It's time to celebrate, to appreciate nature's beauty.

As the rain and sun meet in peace

A rainbow arches in the high, grand and complete

From red to violet, hues so radiant and bright

A breathtaking curve, a colourful delight.

Birds sing out in joy that puts the heart at ease

In the meadows, flowers dance, a fragrance in the breeze

Rain on a sunny day, a lovely sight to behold

Bringing colours, pure delight, a story to be told.

Rain Dance in Forest

Rain falls gently on the hills

Bringing life to all it fills

Soothing music of life and growth

That echoes through the forest both.

Trees reach up to catch the drops

Thirst they quench, their longing stops

They rise, they drink, they grow proud and tall

A cool escapade, a refuge for all.

Raindrops fall upon the ground

Pitter-patter, a happy tapping sound

As they seep quickly into the earth

Gaily they soak the earth with their mirth.

Forest floor becomes alive

With moss and fern so green and thrive

Rain has brought it back to life

Creatures of God here know no pain or strife.

Canopy now filled with gentle mist

A cloak of nature's silent bliss

It swirls and dances in the breeze

Like a web of majesty and intrigue.

As raindrops create a mesmerising sprawl

I stand in awe of their graceful fall

In each drop, a reflection of the sky

A mirror of nature passing by.

Rain on Mountain High

Cascading down with bubbling sound

Rain pours its blessings all around

Nature's rhythm beyond compare

Raindrops dance and sing a melody in the air.

Peaks rejoice in cool embrace

Raindrops kiss the mountain face

Clouds, they cling to every crevice

Fleeting touch, moment's bliss.

Streams and rivers rush to life

Fed by the rain, free from strife

Waterfalls gush through stones and rocks

A grand spectacle to watch.

When rain pours on mountain high

A gift from heavens, from the endless sky

Pine needles glisten, a jewelled display

Wildflowers peek through, reborn this day.

The mountain stands unbowed, unbent

A timeless form, by nature sent

Earth awakens, ready to bestow

Her gift of life, gifts of growth for generations to go.

A Winter Wonderland

Snowflakes fall upon mountain peak
They dance, they twirl in frosty breeze
White trees and mountains stand so proud and tall
Winter's delicate, silent sprawl, a magical thrall.

Fierce wind whistles through valleys deep
Snowdrifts climb up the slope so steep
A frozen landscape so serene and still
A winter wonderland, tranquil and chill.

Snowflakes twirl, spin in the air
A graceful dance of winter's flair
A world so pristine, untouched by time
A place where wild things still roam, and the sun always shines.

High above the world, snow-capped peaks glisten bright

In this pristine domain, earth and sky in harmony white

Mountain range is alive with mystical allure

A place of awe and wonder where the human spirit can soar.

Snowflakes dance upon the mountain's crest

Nature's brushstroke, a wintry bequest

Soft, intricate crystals, each a work of art

Tiny masterpieces, crafted by nature, with precision and heart.

Love in Snow

The world turns into a wonderland, gleaming white and bright

Painting the canvas anew, silently the snowflakes dance

In the crisp, still air, nature's magic takes flight

Beside the frozen lake in this snowy expanse, a perfect place to romance.

Chill in the air is biting

The warmth of their love prevails

As they walk hand in hand, delighting

In the magic that snow unveils.

Snowflakes there, around them dance

As if celebrating their love so true

That moment is filled with joy and trance

Worries gone with winds whistling through.

Snowflakes whisper of longing and love

Like a million tiny kisses from the heavens above

As they fall from the sky

They melt away with a sigh.

In the magical winter wonderland of love unbound

Where snow falls like a gentle embrace

Two hearts drawn together, their laughter brings the warmth around

Their love stands strong in this enchanting place.

Snow keeps falling, they embrace in each other's hold

Forgotten of the world, their hearts beating as one

The world around them is gone

They are one, winter chill is worth its gold.

Crystal Falling

Powerful force, it shakes the ground

With thundering feet and pounding sound

Storm clouds crackle with flashes ultra-bright

Their echoes resound through the night.

In that moment, all is still

Earth holds its breath so chill

A beacon of light in the night

Decorates the darkness with hope and delight.

Thunderclaps so fierce and loud

Sword of lightning parts the dark clouds

Bolts of lightning embrace again and again

In a storm of hail and rain.

Crackling bolts from the heavens high

Paint the sky with ethereal light

Air electrified by every bolt

Composition bright, a divine artist's brush stroke.

Hail descends like crystals falling

In a rhythm, nature's voice is calling

Whispering love message through each icy glance

Calling me in the open air to dance.

Unbridled River

River swells in downpour intense

It's angry, it knows no hindrance

Mad water rushes with a roar that drowns the cry

An unbridled force of nature none can defy.

Water gushes forth, the banks are soon awash

Nature wields its force, so vast and harsh

Torrential flow released, levelling everything in its path

Too much for anyone to match, a force of wrath.

Unimpeded, it flows on and on

The river's wild, free, and strong

Through lush meadows and fields of green

Carves its endless path, a journey anew.

Weaving stories, it meanders through wood's heart

Uncovering wild wonders that have long been kept apart

Majestic forests verdant and lush

Where ancient trees in harmony hush.

River flows with feral grace

Cutting and sculpting landscapes, leaving no space

Nature's artistry in every bend

Eroding coasts, a dance to transcend.

Banks may weather and undergo transformation

They embrace the river's essence, unafraid of mutation

Banks are witness to nature's design sublime

Where harmony and beauty forever intertwine.

Oceanic Fury

In the thick of the angry tempest's junglee roar
A ship is tossed and turned
Its monstrous hull no match for more
Valiant waves cannot be spurned.

Strong winds threaten and lash the sails
Thunder drums its beat, a warning to all
Crew doth struggle to prevail
And keep the ship afloat and tall.

Waves clash, sea doth rage with anger and boom
Calamitous rain pours down in torrents
Waves reach high, ship is lost in endless gloom
Its fate unpredictable, hope it survives rough currents.

Angry sea, turbulent like an unpeaceful womb

A dance of chaos, nature's furious bloom

Crew's strength and courage through years honed

They battle to keep their own.

This oceanic fury, a breathtaking sight

Awe-inspiring, destructive, also a fright

Never-ending cycle, unstoppable, unyielding

Deadly yet beautiful, crashing and creating.

Though the tempest may rage with wrath and furore

Ship will weather it all, that's sure

With billowing sails and white foam trails

It was built to dare and sail.

Wild Sea

Sea, once calm and serene, now churns with fury and force

Waves crash, a tempest scene, day turns into a dreamy remorse

Waves crash higher and higher, their anger unchecked

As the sea becomes a wild and fearsome wreck.

Winds swirl, a ship is tossed, sailors cling on for dear life

Their strength and endurance put to the test, circular storm unleashes its strife

The masts creak and screech in the storm's relentless assault

The sails flap wildly, sailors hold fast.

Sea with all its power and punch

Lashes out upon the shore with a crunch

Its waves crash and break with a roar

A potent force to be reckoned with, for sure.

Thunder booms, lightning strikes, torrential rain falls so thick

Sea rolls, a tumultuous sight, tempest's rage continually persists

Sailors, they ride the waves and sing their song

Their bond stronger than the wind's strength, they fight all night long.

When the storm finally subsides, sun shines once more in the sea

Sailors emerge strong from the depths, inspired

Men of adventure, with a love for the sea, are rewired

Gentle waves kiss the shore, life's beauty we can see.

Tide's Embrace

Towering tidal waves rushing forth distant land

Pounding on shore, crashing on sand

Rushing forward fierce and bold

Power of the ocean, awesome and cold.

A surge of water like a living beast

Devouring the land, its hunger increased

Waves, they thrash and crash, an ocean's dance

A captivating performance, an aqueous romance.

With swash and backwash, they crash and collide

Spraying mist and foam far and wide

Tidal waves, a breathtaking spectacle

Colossal surge, magnificent and unstoppable.

The ebb and flow of the tide's embrace

Bringing hope, then dashing it away

Waves moving, in and out, to and fro

The Beau ocean is drawn to Belle shore.

As the tide begins to retreat

Ocean withdraws gracefully, it does concede

Treading lightly upon the sand

Whispering a secret, kissing the land.

Roaring Cyclone

Waves rise up, like light frothy foam
Wind's eerie tone echoes and moans
In the Bay of Bengal, a cyclone stirs
Whirling wild winds, tall waves it spurs.

With dynamic force, it begins to form
Gathering strength, a cyclone to transform
Boats bob up and down, tossed by the waves
As the cyclone's fury relentlessly raves.

Trees uprooted, buildings crushed
Life disrupted, nature's brutal brush
Roaring cyclone, a fearsome gust
No mercy shown in its wild rush.

With swirling winds and torrential rain
Sky turns darker, into night turns the day
The world is a cacophony of sound
Chaos dances, harmony's drowned.

Ships take shelter as the storm instils fear
Their hulls battle bravely like determined warriors
With each gust, their resolve is tested
Their determination unwavering, never arrested.

People huddle, and fear and dread
Praying for their lives, tears they shed
They pray and pray, their voices rising high
Imploring for respite from the sinister sky.

Tornado Dance

Sea waves crash against the shore

A sound as old as time before

Sky turns dark, air grows cold

As a fierce tornado takes hold.

It spins and twists with deadly force

Turning down cars, razing homes off course

It leaves a trail of devastation

Tornado, it is a perdition.

Seagulls cry overhead

A warning to the fish below

Sandpipers scurry to and fro

A foreboding of what's in store.

It brings destruction in its wake

Leaves a trail of ruin and ache

Unstoppable power that's impossible to be restrained

A force of nature that cannot be contained.

In the midst of this scrambled scene

Beauty of nature can still be seen

Tornado twirls and dances, a wild and angry thing

It spins and spins and spins, a destructive king.

The Day the Sky Opened Up

Monsoon sky above, it opens up and pours
A deluge falls upon the shores
Waves crash against the rocks
Rain breaks down on the docks.

Raging rivers now replace the sand
Nature's fury unleashed, unplanned
The world is beneath this watery weight
Struggles, fights to alter fate.

The tempest's wrath, the heaven's cry
As lightning strikes and thunder is nigh
The world is drenched in water's might
A boogying liquid, a dazzling sight.

As rivers rush, currents grow

A jig of motion, a rhythmic flow

In their magnificent form, currents play

Water's relentless power on display.

Don't give up hope, you'll make

Stay strong through the storm's harshest shake

For nature's ways are wise, don't stop to rest

Your journey is your best.

Amphan

Rising from the depths of the Bay of Bengal

With ferocity and severity, it begins to swell

A rotating storm roars through the darkened sky

Monsoon calls, thunder rumbles high.

Amphan cyclone, a tempest in flight

Aggressive and dreadful monster that ignites

Fear in hearts with its persistent force

Heartbeats falter as chaos sets its course.

Rising and falling, crashing and foaming, the waves enhance

Changing and evolving with each advance

The cyclone marches towards the coastal crowd untamed

A warning to all in its destructive path unnamed.

Screaming, scaring with pounding rain, it comes ashore

Shaken souls tremble at nature's wicked roar

Nimbus clouds clash, creating fears in highs

Darkness looming, shadows dance in eerie guise.

Trees uprooted, rooftops are gone

Streets transformed into rivers, rushing strong

Crops once green and happy, now all battered and forlorn

Floodwaters rampaging where they don't belong.

People flee to seek refuge and hope

Navigating the chaos in cyclone, learning to cope

In makeshift shelters, solace is found

Complete strangers, they huddle together, warmth abound.

Amphan's severe assault, a force of disruption

Leaves behind a vast trail of destruction

Taking away with it dreams, lives, and construction

Yet, from the wreckage, hope will find resurrection.

Folks stand together strong and strive

They'll rebuild their houses and their lives

The cyclone may have left scars

But the human spirit shines like stars.

Nature's Tandav may come and go

Hope and courage will always sow

In the face of challenges, mortals stand together, they all know

Through unity and resilience, they'll grow.

Unleashed

Clouds dark and heavy, pregnant with rain
Gathered in the sky, ready to unleash their pain
Wind is angry, trees begin to sway
Air is thick with tension as the storm begins to play.

Streaks of bright light illuminate the sky
Thunder crashes noisily as the storm's wild cry
As expected, it begins a torrential downpour
Rain beats on the roof like drums and more.

Streets are flooded fast, water rises high
Cars are washed away as the floods begin to ply
Tree-lined riverbanks breached, water rushes by
Intense turbulence released in wild waves' cry.

Water is rising, there's nowhere to go

All running scared, what to do, they don't know

Some are trying to stay afloat

With every ounce of strength they hold.

They press on, against the waves that loom

They tread water, facing the storm's gloom

Undeterred, they chart a resilient path

Finding strength within, they fuel their own hearth.

Clouds finally begin to clear, storm at last abated

Sun breaks through bright, as the storm is dissipated

In its wake, the world is bright and renewed

Air is fresh and clean with life imbued.

Though cloudburst brings destruction and strife

It also brings new beginnings of life

Storm may be dark and scary

It brings light and happiness like the magical wand of a fairy.

When the World Unravels

In the severe storm's savage yowl, big, old trees cry and
bow
Their roots strained with earth's deep growl
Branches thrash and twist as winds furiously plough
Their trunks scarred, leaves torn off the boughs.

Birds gather in the trees, their song silenced
With wings tucked tight, they weather the gale
Beasts seek refuge from nature's fierce array
Until it passes, they'll stay at bay.

Some branches snapped with brittle cracks
Echo through the woods like thunderclaps
Leaves are beaten to the ground
In the storm's wrath, they made no sound.

Stream swollen to a flood rushes madly by

Rocks torn off their bed, wind is rough and high

Life clings to the shore, a struggle to endure

Fighting for a chance to see the sun once more.

Even in their broken state

Fallen trees hold unlimited worth

In their fallen form and final fate

They give new life to soil and earth.

For every leaf and sprig that falls

A new seed will take its place

So the cycle of life calls

New life will rise in grace.

Squall Sweep

In a land where the sky meets the sea
A tempest brews with a fierce decree
Born from the depths of blue water's wrath
It gathers strength along its path.

A swirling force, a high-powered wand
The southeastern cyclone bolts towards the land
It brings chaos, destruction, and woe
There's no way to hide from this furore.

Its eye, a calm, amidst the storm
Deceptive place, a transient form
In its core, turmoil resides
Frenzy at its will, persistent tides.

Winds whiz, and sky turns grey

As the squall sweeps through the Sunderbans Bay

Trees bend and sway as if in a wild romance

But there's no joy here, just a deadly dance.

Water rises inch by inch

As the storm surge crashes and begins to pinch

Wind whips up the water unbound

Lashing violently against the ground.

Rain cascades in a sudden downpour

Devouring the land in its watery hoard

People scramble, seeking higher ground

Hope and pray, they are not drowned.

People here, so brave and strong

Their courage ignites a resounding song

Through trials and tribulations, they persist

With unwavering faith and hope, their bravery insists.

Super Cyclone

A super cyclone, a creature of chaos and flare

A darkness that brings dread and despair

With strong, ultrafast winds that charge with hostility

Can level entire towns and cities.

Waves pound the beach, unrelenting and unforgiving

Drowning out all sound save their own

Wind whips up sand, eyes and skin stinging

Waves crash and free flies the foam.

Mountain like waves know no obstruction

They bring with them death and destruction

People in their path are forced to flee

Leaving behind their homes and families.

In rising water like a giant wave

People drowned, their homes are graves

Their hopes and dreams swept away

Past is buried, all that's left is today.

Trees and plants torn and stripped

Nature's beauty cruelly whipped

Once adorned with vibrant grace

Now left barren, a desolate space.

Cyclone leaves trees uprooted

Leaving nature's beauty upended

Their strong, high branches now defeated

Lie scattered and broken, once splendid.

Once sturdy and strong, they stood kissed by sun rays

Providing shelter to creatures, all in their green embrace

Only emptiness remains, grove in despair

Nature's melody silenced, no vibrant song in the air.

Animals have all fled, birds have taken flight

Leaving behind a world of silence and plight

No sweet sound of nature, no songs to hear

Their absence brings a sorrow so severe.

The sky once vibrant, now veiled in a shade of sombre hue

Yearns for vibrant pigments anew

A world in disarray devoid of its grace

Longing for colours to return and embrace.

No flowers to greet the eyes, only desolate, devoid of light

The ground is a barren sight

Seems like nothing will again ever grow

Earth is strong, she will endure.

A world without colours, a world without breath

Where the sky is ashen and all is death

In the absence of glowing colours, a void descends

Aching for the rainbow, where beauty extends.

In this void, a spark of hope ignites

A realm of wonder where imagination takes flight

Ideation finds its strength, it hones

Awakening visions previously unknown.

Aila

Raging, roaring, soaring over the land

A tempest wild with scale so grand

The superstorm, a dreadful force

A catastrophic upheaval without remorse.

Sky grew dark with clouds so dense

That blocked out sun and all sense

Lightning bolts and echoing thunder cracked open the sky's door

With wind and rain, God's fury poured.

Trees bowed low as if in prayer

Rain fell in torrents, wind whipped through air

Nature's forces clashed, a chilling scene

Frightening power displayed, unseen, extreme.

The ocean swelled with waves so high

They crashed against the shore, nature's battle cry

A child sat behind a rock, embracing the unknown

Unaware of what might come, unafraid to be alone.

The super cyclone swept across the land so fast

No one, no one could flee from its grasp

Day or night, it was all the same

Originating in the Bay of Bengal, Aila was its name.

Storm's mad wrath, a fearsome sight

Ponds and fields, a barren plight

No fish to trawl, no rice to yield

No hope to cling to, no joy to feel.

It brought down houses, shattered dreams

Leaving behind a trail of ruins and screams

Through tears that fell like endless rain

Folks stood strong to rise again.

In the middle of turmoil and despair

There were some who dared to care

They rose up with hearts so brave

To help the weak, save the old and lit the way.

Fallen Banyan

Ancient trees that kissed heavens high

In a land where nature thrived

Where wildlife roamed with grace beside

Stood a grand banyan, tall and wide.

Its roots, like serpents, embraced the earth

Unyielding, strong, a symbol of birth

Its figs were red, nourishing and sweet

A feast for the birds and the bees.

One evil evening, thick apocalyptic clouds loomed

Casting a shadow, sunlight entombed

Sky's serene beauty consumed

Foreboding of an impending doom.

Gale howled angrily, lightning danced

Sky ablaze, earth shocked, the clouds advanced

In the chaotic uproar, firm banyan stood tall

Enduring the wrathful nature's assault.

Dark clouds loomed, their anger clear

As if saying, "Beware, we are here"

Cold winds threatened, sky turned grey

Nature's stage prepared for a tempest's play.

As the storm grew stronger, fiercer still

Wind lashed wildly with a vengeful thrill

Ancient giant once proud and tall

Began to swing vehemently, its strength in thrall.

Rumbles echoed through the night of doom

As the banyan fought with all its fumes

Alas! A storm so fierce it could not withstand

In a deafening crash, the giant fell, as if by command.

The ground trembled as if in sorrow

For a fallen guardian and its own morrow

Fallen banyan tree lay shattered in a heap

Beneath its weight, the earth did weep.

Even in its collapse, its beauty thrived

A poignant reminder that hope will survive

Though the leaves may fall, trunk may break

Roots will still be there, they'll not forsake.

Storm Tossed

Lost in the midst of a violent storm
I battle to find my way
Strong winds whistle, rain beats down
I lurch through the fray.

As I wander through the dark, lonely night
I long for a guiding light
I can't see moon nor shining stars
My soul is lost, heavy is heart.

Darkness seems to cover me all
I struggle through the rain
Can't see a beam of light, I trip and fall
I fear I'll never find my way home again.

A thunder echoes with all its height

My eyes are closed, my mind takes flight

I press on through the rain and wind

I'm drenched, I'll not give in.

Even in the depth of a storm so fierce

I hear a still small voice

Whispering softly in my ears

Let happiness be your choice.

Through the violent storm

I know I'll find my way

Breaking the deep darkness

I'll reach the light of a beaming, clear day.

The storm may batter me

May shake me from head to knee

I'll hold my ground without fright

Till I come out stronger in light.

The Dance of Nature's Fury

Sky turns red with anger
A dust storm is brewing in the air
Wind begins to whistle, surroundings tremble
The world is dark and full of fear.

Air grows thick with dust
Sand is whipped about
Trees bend low in fear
As the storm begins to shout.

The sun is hidden behind a veil
Darkness descends, the world turns pale
Day turns to a hazy night
A shroud of dust, a blinding sight.

As the storm gets closer, winds unfurl

Whispering tales of danger, they hurl

Wings beat wildly, against the turbulent tide

Birds take flight in terror, seeking refuge to hide.

Animals all hide away

In their homes, safe, and bow in prayer

Scattered like ants, people run for their life

All in a panic, they try to survive.

Wind picks up its pace and speed

A force that no one can impede

Dust swirls, relentless and strong

Obscuring the world, where it belongs.

It tosses everything in sight

Whirling tempest of sandy haze

Engulfing the land in a fiery blaze

A fearsome sight, a chilling fright.

Through the chaos, a resilient plea

For calm to return, for peace to be free

Until then, the dust storm prevails

Unyielding and fierce, as nature entails.

The storm rages on and on

A battle that seems never gone

Until the wind begins to wane

Dust begins to settle again.

Turbulence

A turbulence in my mind is seething
Whipping up thoughts, emotions engaging
Anxiety bolts, they strike and sear
Thunder echoes of doubts and fears.

Dark clouds of confusion cover the mind's expanse
In the fog's embrace, a mystic dance
Torrents of thoughts and feelings, like overwhelming tide
Thrashing my soul, they crash and collide.

In the rain of pain, drowns my soul
In the deluge's grasp, I lose control
Swirling mind, chaos all around
Lost in the inundation that knows no bound.

With the downpour, tears cascade

A deluge of emotions, memories replayed

Through highs and lows, their course is made

A fusion of joy and sorrow, a storm portrayed.

Faces and places long since gone

In darkness, pictures of the past appear

With stories that still linger on

Lost echoes whisper, memories draw near.

I'm swept away, struggling to find my way

Adrift in the vastness, I still hold the sway

I try to hold on to my sanity

In the storm's ferity, I seek clarity.

There's a stillness deep inside

A quiet strength begins to rise

In the clouds of uncertainty, I look for light

A flash of beacon shining bright.

In the haze of tumult and turmoil, a voice I hear

That guides me like a compass through the drear

Through the chaos and doubt, I'll brave the fray

To rise above the tides and reach the peep of day.

www.ingramcontent.com/pod-product-compliance
Lightning Source LLC
Chambersburg PA
CBHW031454130726
47989CB00003B/1382

9 798889 519862 9